Vivaldi Movements from...

THE FOUR SEASONS

Selected and arranged for violin and piano by Jerry Lanning

NIGEL KENNEDY

Chester Music

A NOTE TO THIS EDITION

Vivaldi was an incredibly prolific composer.
He wrote over 500 concertos, more than 230 of them for violin.
The first four of the twelve concertos comprising his Opus 8,
which was published in 1725 with the title
'Il Cimento dell' Armonia e dell' Invenzione'
('The Contest of Harmony and Invention') are amongst the
most popular works in the entire classical repertoire.
They are known to us as 'The Four Seasons'.

Each concerto is prefaced by a sonnet, presumed to be
by Vivaldi himself, which provides a 'programme' for the music.
The sections of the sonnets are initialled, and the initials are
repeated in the music at the appropriate points, so that a direct
relationship between words and music is established.

The four concerti each contain three movements,
making a total of twelve in all. So as to make this edition
suitable for the player of average ability, seven of
the most popular have been specially selected and arranged.

Keys have been simplified in some cases and a few of the more
difficult sections have been cut, although the two slow movements
(Summer II and Winter II) appear in their entirety.

Exclusive distributors:
Chester Music
Newmarket Road, Bury St. Edmunds
Suffolk IP33 3YB.

This book © Copyright 1990 by Chester Music
Order No.CH59055
ISBN 0.7119.2396.5

Photographs courtesy of
London Features International Rex Features

Printed and bound in Great Britain by
Caligraving Limited Thetford Norfolk

Spring I

(Original key: E major)
Antonio Vivaldi
arranged by Jerry Lanning

Allegro

Spring III

Danza Pastorale

(Original key: E major)

Summer II

Autumn I

Autumn III

Winter II

(Original key: Eb major)

Largo

Winter III

(Original key: F minor)

10/96 (26065)